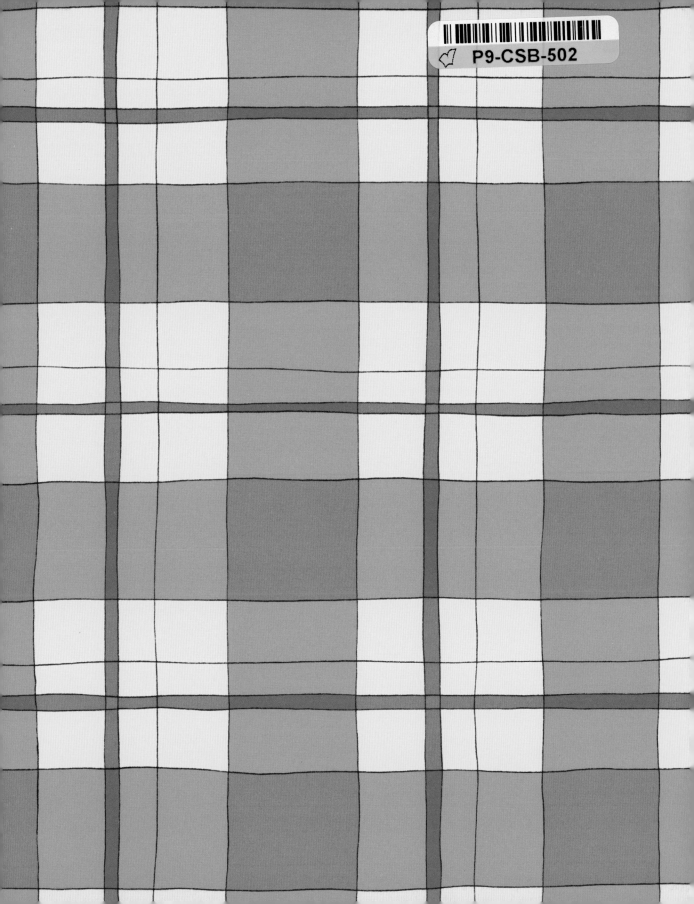

Little People, BIG DREAMS
ANNE FRANK

Written by
Mª Isabel Sánchez Vegara

Illustrated by
Sveta Dorosheva

Lincoln
Children's Books

Anne was a little Jewish girl who was born in
Germany. She lived happily with her parents,
and her older sister, Margot, in the city of Frankfurt.

But when she was four, an ugly man with a little black mustache became the leader of her country. His name was Hitler. He hated the Jews and wanted them to disappear.

Anne's family moved away to Holland, which was a free country. Anne's father opened a business, and they had a home where they felt safe.

But one day, the Nazis invaded half of Europe and arrived in Holland. Anne and all the other Jewish children were forced to go to separate schools and wear a star on their chest.

For her 13th birthday, Anne's parents gave her a diary. That day she discovered the pleasure of writing on her own.

Anne wrote in her diary about how her family lived in fear of being arrested. They decided to leave their home, and move to a secret annex behind a bookshelf at the building where her father worked.

They had to share their tiny new home with another Jewish family and stay very quiet. They could not leave their hiding place, in case anyone found them.

Anne's diary kept her company, and she wrote in it for hours. She wanted to publish a book and become a famous writer.

But one day, Anne stopped writing. The Nazi soldiers had found them, and they were all arrested. Anne's diary was left behind in her room.

The family was pushed onto a train full of
people on its way to a concentration camp.
It took three long days for them to arrive
at the worst place on Earth.

Anne's father, Otto, was the only member of the family
to survive the terrible war. He found her diary and wept
as he read what his young daughter had written.

He decided to publish the diary, and share
Anne's story, just as she would have wanted.
The world had to know the true story.

Since then, millions of people have read and cried over *The Diary of Anne Frank*, the story of the little girl who dreamt of a better world.

ANNE FRANK

(Born 1929 • Died 1945)

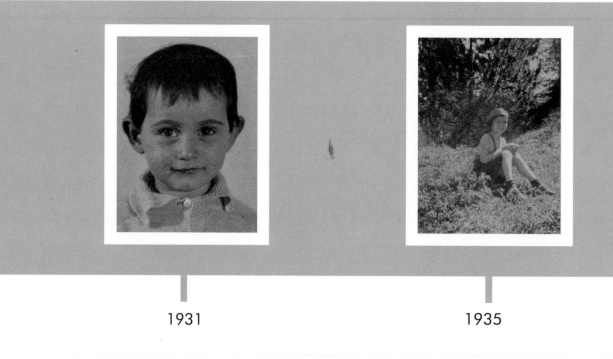

1931   1935

Annelies Frank was born in Germany to a happy family. But when she was four, a cruel government, called the Nazi Party, came into power. It was led by a man named Adolf Hitler, a dictator who forced Germans to follow his unjust rule. The Nazis hated many races, especially Jews, and brought in discriminatory rules against them. Anne's family had to move to Holland in order to be safe. But in 1939, the Nazi Party started World War II, and began invading other countries—including Holland. In 1942, things got worse, and the Frank family had to go into hiding. They hid in a secret annex, tucked behind a bookshelf at Otto Frank's work. They hoped they wouldn't be arrested. Here, Anne kept a diary.

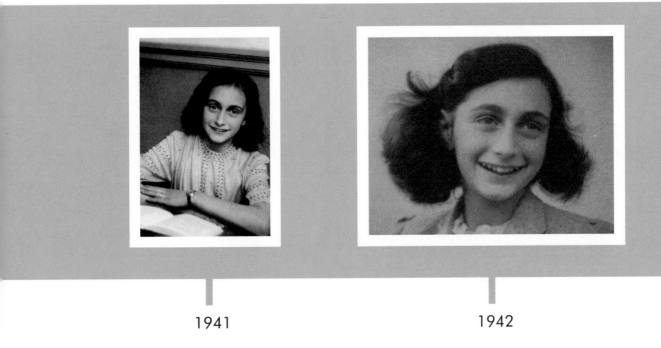

1941   1942

She wanted to tell her story of the war and for people to read it.
In 1944, German police broke into the annex and arrested Anne's
family. They were all sent to concentration camps. Concentration
camps were prisons where many Jews were forced to work. There
was little food and lots of people, and disease spread quickly. Most
people did not survive. Anne died at the Bergen-Belsen camp in
1945, weeks before it was freed by Allied forces. After the war,
Otto found her diary and published her story, as she would have
wanted. Anne became one of the most loved diarists in the world,
and captured the hearts and minds of the public. She lives on
through her words and in all those who read her story.

Want to find out more about **Anne Frank?**
Read one of these great books:

The Diary of a Young Girl by Anne Frank
Who Was Anne Frank? by Ann Abramson and Nancy Harrison
Famous People, Famous Lives: Anne Frank by Harriet Castor
DK: The Story of Anne Frank by Brenda Ralph Lewis

If you're in Amsterdam, you could even visit the Anne Frank Museum—
where Anne lived in secret and wrote her diary.

Brimming with creative inspiration, how-to projects, and useful information to enrich your everyday life, Quarto Knows is a favorite destination for those pursuing their interests and passions. Visit our site and dig deeper with our books into your area of interest: Quarto Creates, Quarto Cooks, Quarto Homes, Quarto Lives, Quarto Drives, Quarto Explores, Quarto Gifts, or Quarto Kids.

Text © 2018 Mª Isabel Sánchez Vegara. Illustrations © 2018 Sveta Dorosheva.
First Published in the UK in 2018 by Lincoln Children's Books, an imprint of The Quarto Group.
400 First Avenue North, Suite 400, Minneapolis, MN 55401, USA.
T (612) 344-8100 F (612) 344-8692 www.QuartoKnows.com
First Published in Spain in 2018 under the title Pequeña & Grande Anne Frank
by Alba Editorial, s.l.u., Baixada de Sant Miquel, 1, 08002 Barcelona
www.albaeditorial.es
All rights reserved.
Published by arrangement with Alba Editorial, s.l.u. Translation rights arranged by IMC Agència Literària, SL
All rights reserved.

ISBN 978-1-78603-229-4

The illustrations were created by hand with nib pen and ink, and watercolor. Set in Futura BT.

Published by Rachel Williams • Designed by Karissa Santos
Edited by Katy Flint • Production by Jenny Cundill

Manufactured in Guangdong, China CC052018

9 7 5 3 1 2 4 6 8

Photographic acknowledgments (pages 28–29, from left to right) 1. Anne Frank at Two, 1931 © Anne Frank Fonds Basel / Getty Images
2. Anne in Switzerland, 1935 © Anne Frank Fonds Basel / Getty Images 3. Anne Frank, 1941 © Anne Frank Fonds Basel / Getty Images
4. Anne Frank, 1942, Photo Collection Anne Frank House, Amsterdam, Public Domain Work

Also in the *Little People,* **BIG DREAMS** series:

FRIDA KAHLO

ISBN: 978-1-84780-783-0

Meet Frida Kahlo, one of the best artists of the twentieth century.

COCO CHANEL

ISBN: 978-1-84780-784-7

Discover the life of Coco Chanel, the famous fashion designer.

MAYA ANGELOU

ISBN: 978-1-84780-889-9

Read about Maya Angelou—one of the world's most beloved writers.

AMELIA EARHART

ISBN: 978-1-84780-888-2

Learn about Amelia Earhart—the first female to fly solo over the Atlantic.

AGATHA CHRISTIE

ISBN: 978-1-78603-220-1

Meet the queen of the imaginative mystery—Agatha Christie.

MARIE CURIE

ISBN: 978-1-84780-962-9

Be introduced to Marie Curie, the Nobel Prize–winning scientist.

ROSA PARKS

ISBN: 978-1-78603-018-4

Discover the life of Rosa Parks, the first lady of the civil rights movement.

AUDREY HEPBURN

ISBN: 978-1-78603-053-5

Learn about the iconic actress and humanitarian—Audrey Hepburn.

EMMELINE PANKHURST

ISBN: 978-1-78603-020-7

Meet Emmeline Pankhurst, the suffragette who helped women get the vote.

ELLA FITZGERALD

ISBN: 978-1-78603-087-0

Meet Ella Fitzgerald, the pioneering jazz singer and musician.

ADA LOVELACE

ISBN: 978-1-78603-076-4

Read all about Ada Lovelace, the first computer programmer.

GEORGIA O'KEEFFE

ISBN: 978-1-78603-122-8

Discover the life of Georgia O'Keeffe, the famous American painter.

HARRIET TUBMAN

ISBN: 978-1-78603-227-0

Learn about Harriet Tubman, who led hundreds of slaves to freedom.

MOTHER TERESA

ISBN: 978-1-78603-230-0

Meet Mother Teresa, the Roman Catholic nun who helped people in need.

JOSEPHINE BAKER

ISBN: 978-1-78603-228-7

Meet Josephine Baker, the dancer, movie star, spy, and activist.